communicating with people:
the supervisor's introduction to verbal communication and decision-making

communicating with people:

the supervisor's introduction to verbal communication and decision-making

RAYMOND J. BURBY, 1916 –

McDonnell-Douglas Corporation
Long Beach, California

ADDISON-WESLEY PUBLISHING COMPANY
Reading, Massachusetts
Menlo Park, California · London · Don Mills, Ontario

This book is in the

ADDISON-WESLEY SERIES IN SUPERVISORY TRAINING

*This book is dedicated
to C. L. Nunnelly
whose insights and encouragement
have lent much to the development of
the thoughts expressed in the text.*

preface

The purpose of this book is to enable you to understand what lies below the surface aspects when people talk to each other. A great many on-the-job decisions are based on verbal discourse. For this reason, all supervisors and managers should have a sound understanding of the communication process.

Some of our ideas are speculative because, of course, we cannot see into people's minds. The various concepts, however, will lead you to a fresh way of thinking about *what we say* or *how we react to what is said to us*. The first three chapters of this book dealing with the verbal communication emphasize what takes place in a person's mind when he is the speaker and also when he is the listener. This material provides the background. Subsequent chapters are work-oriented and illustrate how verbal communication opens or closes doors to understanding.

Examples used in the text are nontechnical. As you read this book you are encouraged to think about some of the examples and illustrations in terms of your *own* experiences. In this way, what you learn will have added meaning for you. We hope you find this book useful and instructive.

contents

how to use this book

This is a programmed text. It is also in the form of a "scramble book" which is fun to work with. You select an answer to a question and then *turn to the page indicated after your answer.*

If you select the right answer, you will be given new material to learn and, in most instances, a new question and a new set of possible answers from which to choose. If you select the wrong answer, you will find out why the answer is wrong, and you will be asked to return to the original page to choose a better answer.

At the top of each answer page you will find, in parentheses, the number of the page on which the question appeared. This will help you find your way back and forth in the book.

How to use this book

CHAPTER 1

the intent to communicate

This book is designed to develop your understanding of *spoken communication*. Most information about the day's work is communicated verbally, either between two people from questions and answers or from discussions of problems, methods, or procedures, or among several people at group or staff meetings.

Since most on-the-job decisions and instructions are given orally and are based upon face-to-face discussions, it follows that the conduct of the business will be greatly improved with an increased understanding of what is happening when spoken communication between people takes place. Once a feel has been developed for these underlying factors, we can evaluate statements more intelligently. We can learn how to get and use feedback and how to make conversation easy. We will become sensitive to some of the thinking behind what is being said.

1

Why do we communicate? Some say, "In order to survive!" Perhaps we communicate to explain something, or to relate the present to the past, or to describe a future course of action. Whatever the reason, we can make one basic assumption: *Communication which has a meaning or purpose is usually preceded by an intention.* Which of the following would you say *best* represents this thought?

1. A speaker's intention could be to change my behavior.
    . . . . Page 4

2. A speaker's intention could be to go fishing. . .Page 5

3. Both of these. . . . . .Page 6

Did you read page xi, "How to Use This Book"? Caution! You are probably so used to turning to the next page while reading a book that you did it quite naturally this time.

This book doesn't work that way. Instead, each time you answer a question, you should proceed directly to the page that is indicated beside your answer.

You answered 1. A speaker's intention could be to change my behavior.

This certainly could be right. But you must realize our question did not delve into specific intentions. Going fishing could be properly classified as an intention of a speaker just as changing my behavior could be his intention.

▲   Please return to page 2 and select a better answer.

You answered 2. A speaker's intention could be to go fishing.

So it could. But you must admit, a speaker's intention could be to change your behavior. So either fishing or changing your behavior could be an acceptable answer to the question.

▲   Please return to page 2 and try again.

You chose 3. Both of these.

This is correct.

Behind *meaningful* communication directed towards you is some intention of the speaker. This intention does not necessarily have to be thought about beforehand. For instance, the speaker might retell a past good or bad experience with the intent of gaining sympathy or pleasure from your reaction. The speaker can do this without having thought about his intent before speaking.

So the intention of a communication (from now on when you read "communication" it will mean spoken communication) can take many forms. The speaker may be trying to get to the root of a situation. Many conversations are an exchange of words where the intention is to determine the truth about something. Or the speaker may be trying to change the listener's beliefs or behavior. He could be attempting to get some kind of reaction or feedback from the listener to support his own feeling of security or well-being. The speaker's intention, whether arrived at consciously or unconsciously, can also be a combination of things such as both getting your attention and making sure you understand the communication.

Suppose a company with twenty thousand employees provides assigned parking spots to those in a management position. All other employees use a general parking area on a first-come, first-served basis. Alex is a supervisor and is planning a week's business trip. One of the employees working for Alex asks him, "Are you planning to be out of town all next week?" Alex feels there could be many reasons for such a question. So he answers, "Yes. Is there any problem?" The employee says, "No, I just want to use your parking spot if you won't be using it."

This is a simple illustration of a typical conversation initiated by a speaker with a pre-determined intent. We say typical because it is not unusual for someone to start a conversation based on some intent completely unknown to the listener.

Though conversations can take many forms, we will generalize and place them in two categories: One we will call *social-type conversations;* the other, *business-type conversations.*

Social conversations are communications such as gossiping, recounting weekend experiences, telling jokes, or exchanging generalized viewpoints. Such conversations help people to relate with one another and are necessary to a balanced existence. Business conversations are specific communications which are work-related.

▲   Now turn to page 8.

Please read the following statements and see whether you can
determine which are most likely social-type statements and
which are probably business-type statements.

a) "I would like Bill and John to check in early tomorrow
    so we can finish the job."
b) "You should have seen those two after I showed them
    the picture."
c) "I felt O.K. until the pain-killer wore off."
d) "We'll have to do this all over. The whole lot is rejected."

Select your answer from the choices below.

1. Both (a) and (b) are social type statements; (c) and (d),
    business-type . . . . Page 9

2. The business-type statements are (a) and (d); social-type,
    (b) and (c). . . . . .Page 10

3. I select (a), (b), and (c) as social-type statements, (d) as a
    business-type statement. . . . . .Page 12

You answered 1. Both (a) and (b) are social-type statements; (c) and (d), business-type.

Perhaps you missed the point of this question.

We are trying to sort out which statements you would expect to hear from a supervisor or in a work situation, and which you would expect in a social-type situation.

▲   Please return to page 8 and try again.

2. The business-type statements are (a) and (d); the social-type, (b) and (c).

Yes, this is the best answer.

There was a good reason behind this little exercise. We must recognize that a certain amount of on-the-job conversations are social. People have a need to relate with one another. The fact that they are at work doesn't turn this off.

All of us can usually tell when a conversation is social in nature. In this book we will discard social conversations from our thinking; we will concern ourselves only with conversations which pertain to the work situation. These are the communications which deal directly with getting work done and indirectly with the work environment. They may include, for example, suggestions, complaints, and a host of other verbalizations associated with the business function.

Earlier we said a possible reason for communicating was to get to the root of a matter, in other words, to determine the truth about something. In most instances we can determine the truth about something only when proper communication takes place. Here's an example:

An analyst from the production planning department conducted a time study and concluded that a collection of outsize parts could be loaded on pallets in a different way which would save time, thus money. Pallets were being loaded on a hit-or-miss basis, resulting in inefficient stacking. Furthermore, moving the pallets was tricky because of unstable loads. The analyst reasoned that if two pallets were loaded at about the same time, the loader would be able to decide how the various sizes of parts could best be loaded. He could then load the parts of a similar size on the same pallet.

The planning analyst estimated the savings involved, and told the supervisor about his calculations. The supervisor agreed with the idea and directed the production planning department to change both the loading procedure and the job cost estimates. In turn, the supervisor of the loading group told all his men the system had been changed. They were to load two pallets at a time instead of one at a time.

Instead of saving time, however, loading two pallets at once took as long as loading them one at a time and the loads were still unstable. Whose fault was this?

Your choice was 3. I select (a), (b), and (c) as social-type statements; (d) as a business-type statement.

You came close. Remember, we are trying to sort out those statements which you would expect to hear in a work situation from those which have to do with the work.

▲ Please return and try again.

You chose 1. The production planning analyst. Uh, uh.

The analyst had a good idea, that's for sure. However, the value of the idea and the possible savings to the company could be proved only after some trial experiments. The conclusion arrived at by the analyst was in error: A number of factors had been overlooked. In this sense he was to blame. But don't you feel that the others involved in the decision process were also at fault?

▲   Please return and select the correct answer.

2. The production planning supervisor. No.

The analyst had a good idea, but it needed a few trial runs to prove whether or not time would be saved. Both the analyst and the supervisor should have recommended a tryout. So each should share some of the blame.

▲ Please return to page 11 and select a better answer.

3. The loading group supervisor.

Yes, some of the blame must fall on the supervisor. He was closest to the situation and should have been more aware of technical operating problems. Possibly his opinion would not have been welcome, however, and possibly communication channels in the company were not geared to make an exchange of ideas easy.

The analyst had a good idea, but it needed a few trial runs to prove whether or not time would be saved. In this sense, both the analyst and the production planning supervisor should have recommended a tryout.

▲   Please return and select a better answer.

You selected 4. In a sense, all three men.

Excellent choice!

You could pin some of the blame upon any one of those involved with the decision. Often too much energy is expended fixing blame, however. The plain fact is that the feasibility of the plan was never soundly established, nor was communication adequate. Had the pallet-loading idea been tested, had each of the three responsible persons been in proper communication, and had proper instructions been given to the pallet loaders, the results would have been far more satisfactory.

This example demonstrates another problem which may arise when we try to get to the root of things. See whether you can determine what was demonstrated, by selecting the better of the following statements.

1. We tend to believe what we hear.   . . . . Page 18
2. Nobody should believe anything he hears unless he has real proof.   . . . . Page 20

PeoPLe Tend to BeLieve What They Hear...

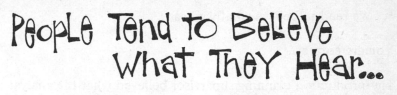

'YOU DON'T LOOK WELL'

1. We tend to believe what we hear.

You are correct.

The production planning supervisor believed what the analyst said about his time-saving idea. The supervisor of the loading group believed his instructions without questioning the validity of the reasoning behind the instructions.

You understand, of course, that the loading problem under-scores the value of pooling communication so that the experience and intelligence of all concerned can be brought to bear on an idea.

What actually happened in this case can be described briefly as follows: The analyst ran a series of tests on the proposed idea and found that the incompatible parts could remain un-loaded through three pallets. By this time enough of these parts would accumulate so that they could be loaded quickly and with more stability on a fourth pallet. In this way the analyst did demonstrate that savings were possible; he did develop a new loading technique which could be passed along to the loading group. However, this was not what he had originally planned.

▲   Go now to page 19.

The following are some review questions on the subject of "The Intent to Communicate." See how well you can do with these questions! Here is the first one. Which of the following is a true statement?

1. Most day-by-day decisions are based on verbal conversations. . . . . Page 21

2. Most day-by-day decisions are based on written information. . . . . Page 22

You selected 2. Nobody should believe anything he hears unless he has real proof.

The production analyst's report of his new stacking idea, and the supervisor's acceptance of the idea is an example of believing what we hear without question. The supervisor, of course, had no proof that the proposal would produce the desired results. It is not at all unusual for people to act upon information this way; people tend to believe what they hear, especially from those in whom they have confidence.

There is really nothing wrong with this providing one has the ability to sense and look deeper into matters which might jeopardize the job (or even the business) if a bad decision is made.

▲ Please return and select the other answer.

1. Most day-by-day decisions are based on verbal conversations.

You are correct.

The decisions reached as a result of discussing problems out-
number by far those based on written analyses. This observation carries even more weight when you realize that most
written determinations originate from a verbal exchange of
some kind.

It was stated that behind a spoken communication which has
a meaning or purpose is some intent on the part of the
speaker. Choose the right answer from the following statements.

2. Most day-by-day decisions are based on written information.

We don't agree with this answer. Most very important
business decisions are based upon studies, reports, and other
written materials, of course. But these are small in number
indeed when compared to the "let's do it that way" decisions
which are part of every day's work.

▲   Please return to page 21 and follow through with the
correct answer.

You answered 1: The speaker may or may not be aware of the real intention behind his communication.

This is correct.

The speaker can be fully aware of his reason or intent for making a statement. Conversely, the speaker can say things without really having analyzed or thought about his intentions. An example could be an emotional outburst aimed at swaying another person's judgment. Chances are the outburst rolls out without the speaker's being aware of his precise intentions.

Since, as we noted, there were generally two types of communications, social or business, we can expect to find during work hours:

1. Nothing but business-type conversations. . . . Page 26
2. A certain amount of both business and social conversation. . . . . Page 27

Your answer was 2: The speaker is never really aware of his intentions.

Whatever gave you that idea?

Do you remember the example of the chap who wanted to use his boss's parking spot? This person's intention was specific, and he sure knew what he wanted. We make the assumption that a person usually knows what he wants and why he acts as he does. There are times, of course, when his intentions are masked either because he doesn't understand his own motives or simply because he hasn't thought about them.

▲   Now please return to page 23 for your third question.

You selected 3. The intent of the speaker is always a conscious one. In other words, the speaker is always aware of the intent of his communications.

This is a most unusual speaker!

Consider the person who tries to prove the validity of a position he has taken on some subject. His intention might be to prove he's right. But another intention which he hasn't considered, because it was masked, is to make you appreciate his intellect.

Situations have a way of causing people to react without examining their intentions. Perhaps this kind of reaction comes because we have learned certain responses and make them automatically. We don't stop to question whether they are right or wrong at the time, or whether these responses correctly satisfy our intentions.

▲ Please return to page 23 for your review and third question.

1. Nothing but business-type conversations.

We don't believe you really meant to make this response. You may remember we narrowed verbal communicating down to two types: social or business. Please don't assume that because a person is at work, all conversations are business conversations.

During working hours, people talk about many social things of interest to them. They talk about golf, the movies, week-end or evening happenings, for example.

▲ Please proceed to page 27 for your last question.

You chose 2: A certain amount of both business and social conversations.

This is correct.

People have a need to socialize with one another, even during business hours. You can depend on the fact that everyone spends a certain amount of time each day discussing matters which have nothing to do with his work. Please remember, however, that we plan to study ideas about *only those spoken communications that deal with the work situation.*

Here is a final question to answer before you proceed to the next chapter.

Do you believe that truth, if known, is obtainable by anyone providing it can be communicated?

1. Absolutely not!   .   .   .   . Page 28
2. Certainly!   .   .   .   .   . Page 29

1. Absolutely not!

A great deal of all human problems lie at the door of communication difficulties. We would like you to feel that the truth about anything is obtainable, providing it is known and can be communicated. Sometimes, even when the truth is known, the communication channels for transmitting the facts are blocked by such things as misinterpretation of the message or by disturbed emotions which drive away meaningful communication.

▲ Please proceed to page 30 and Chapter 2, "The Act of Communication."

You say 2: Certainly!

We're with you!

A great many human problems lie at the door of communication difficulties. One of the problems is that the truth is often lost when statements and conclusions are based on incomplete data, misconception of facts, or hastiness and jumping to conclusions.

▲   Please proceed to page 30 and Chapter 2, "The Act of Communication."

CHAPTER 2

the act of communication

Let's examine ways in which your desire to communicate can be fulfilled. From the illustration on the next page, you should be able to determine the ways we use to express ourselves, the ways which result in a communication output.

Obviously, the illustration oversimplifies the communication process. What it says is that once we decide to communicate, we choose one of three paths: we can express ourselves through speaking, through actions, or through the use of symbols. Usually we think, subconsciously and most rapidly, of the possible paths we can take, rationalize our choice, and then act upon our decision. This type of thinking can be called *mental rehearsal*. Communications of all kinds have first a form, then a certain amount of content. We can begin to understand much about the meaning of a communication we receive if we can first become sensitive to the content,

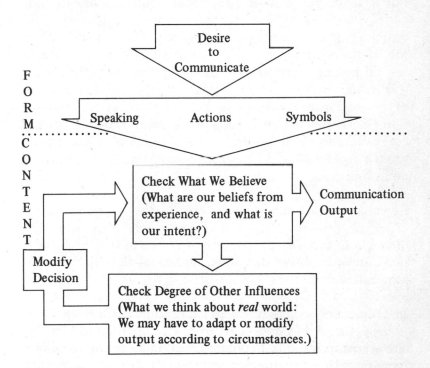

and then try to get a feeling as to the reason for the form selected by the communicator.

If we hesitate before making the communication, it's usually because during the rehearsal we may get second thoughts. We may not continue to believe in the advantage of what was selected as the initial form or content of the intended output.

For instance, you may have repeatedly requested one of your employees to keep the top of his workbench neat and orderly. On this occasion, you happen to pass by and find the top of the workbench completely cluttered. You decide to remind him again; on second thought, you sweep the clutter to the floor with an outraged swipe of your arm. The content of the action is the same as that for a verbal communication—the desire for an orderly work area. The form of the communication is more dramatic—a rejection of the use of spoken requests and a clattering demonstration expressing a desire and need.

Research into human behavior tells us there are three basic drives or pressures which underlie people's behavior: the drive (1) to survive, (2) to reproduce, and (3) to gain recognition. We feel another one could be added—the drive to communicate.

In early childhood the desire to express himself is given direction by the child's awareness of the things around him. He also learns to respond to communication by acting according to the coaxing of parents or others. Of course, subsequent contact with his environment, in and out of school, keeps refining this ability to take part in what we might call two-way communication. The process of communication is such a necessary and constant ingredient of living that we tend to act upon, or react to, communication without giving much thought as to what transpires when we speak with each other.

Let us pause here a minute and examine the words "ball" and "pretty ball." The word "ball" describes an object, but the word "pretty" is interpretive of a *feeling* towards the object.

Now, from this example, do you suppose early learning about communicating with others begins with

1. Learning descriptive words?   .   .   .   .   .   .   Page 34
2. Learning interpretations, relationships?   .   .   Page 37

You answered 1: Learning descriptive words.

You are correct.

Effective verbal communication starts with learning the words which identify things such as shoes or toys. A child learns the words for nose, toe, shoe, sox, and so forth.

Although he may first be conscious of a relationship—for example, this little thing on that other thing can wiggle—he cannot verbally communicate until he has learned the word

for the wiggling thing, *toe,* and the other thing, *foot.* Interpretive words, "pretty," for instance, or "huge" and "tiny," come later with the learning of discriminations.

By the time a person reaches his teens or becomes an adult, most others assume such a person has learned to identify with his surroundings and has the ability to make logical discriminations. The communication process has become more complicated. By the time he approaches adulthood, the way he acts and reacts to situations is an outgrowth of his own particular life experiences. While all of us use the same physical communication processes, our reaction to any given situation and our selection of form or content varies.

We no longer are dealing with childlike concepts and discoveries. We are communicating on an adult level which involves the tremendous backlog of experiences, beliefs, and interpretations which make up our reservoir of learnings.

Each individual's background is unique. Each of countless inputs has been stored and related to others in very special ways; the total impact of experience on one person is unlike that on anyone else. When you think about the wide range of possible social and ethnic backgrounds, and the innumerable combinations of personal experiences possible even within a limited environment, you begin to understand the enormous range of individual differences. To communicate successfully, we have to make assumptions about these ingredients—the individual experiences which determine our own points of view and those which have influenced the other person.

Which of the statements below do you feel best expresses your general belief about people with whom you come into contact?

1. I think people are different, and therefore they do not use the same communicating processes I use.   . Page 38
2. I feel most people probably have the same communication processes I possess.   . . . . Page 39

2. Learning interpretations, relationships.

No, this is incorrect.

While a very young child may be able to see and understand the relationship between his thumb and mouth, he cannot communicate to us what he thinks. First he needs words which mean the appendage called a thumb and the opening in the head called a mouth, and then words to express what his thoughts may be about them.

▲   Please return and select the other answer.

You chose 1: I think people are different, and therefore they do not use the same communicating processes I use.

Well, while it's true people differ somewhat in their appearance and in their learning experiences, they do not differ in the physical processes used to communicate. We all use a similar communication system of mind, nerves, muscles, and vocal chords.

▲ Please return and select the correct response.

Your choice was 2: I feel most people probably have the same communication processes I possess.

You are correct.

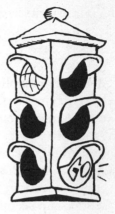

You recognized that while people have different reservoirs of experience, all of us are equipped with a faculty to think and to convey our thoughts. The form with which we choose to express ourselves and the decisions we make are dependent upon the nature of our learning experiences and our capacity to think and reason.

You made an important discrimination when you chose the second statement as the more probable.

The next step is to examine what takes place when people talk to each other. Let's say that A is motivated to speak to B. Right away we should visualize a communication *network*. With this network in mind, can you give priority to one of the following?

1. First we must have a sender and a receiver. . . Page 40
2. First we must have thoughts which, as a sender, we want to convey.   .   .   .   . Page 42
3. You've lost me on this question.   .   .   .   . Page 43

Your priority was 1: A sender and receiver.

This is correct.

A network implies a combination of things tied together. We were trying to convey the concept of *two* persons communicating.

In earlier discussions we identified the two persons as the speaker and the listener. As soon as the listener hears the communication, the roles change. The listener becomes the sender and so on. In order to help you understand the communication process, we will illustrate what is transpiring.

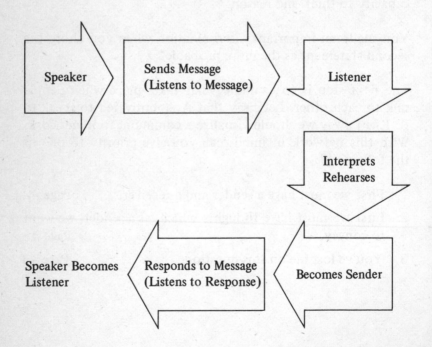

From this diagram we see that a communication between two people involves several things. The most obvious is that there is a message communicator (or sender) and a message recipient (or receiver). We can also see that these roles change. This then, is an example of interaction involving both audio and visual components. There may, of course, be a spin-off at some point if and when one participant decides to take action.

Consider the role of the sender of a communication in a work environment, and try to determine what goes through his mind *before* a message is sent. Please select the most likely statement about what happens before a message is sent.

1. The sender is motivated to say something, not necessarily giving the message any "pre-thought."   .   .   . Page 44

2. The sender probably has a reason for his message and therefore sends it spontaneously with no extra to-do.
   .   .   .   . Page 45

3. Chances are the sender of a message rehearses the message to himself before uttering one word.   .   .   .   .   . Page 46

You answered 2: First we must have thoughts which, as a sender, we want to convey.

You overlooked one thing: to communicate means to send and receive messages. While it is true we must have thoughts in order to do this, communication cannot take place without a sender and receiver.

▲   Please return and try again.

You answered 3. You've lost me on this question.

O.K. We are discussing the concepts which have to do with people's talking back and forth with one another. Usually a person thinks over a message before saying it. But this person has to have someone to hear the message before communication can take place. Thus, the first ingredient is the existence of a sender and receiver.

▲   Please return and try to select the correct answer.

You selected 1: The sender is motivated to say something, not necessarily giving the message any "pre-thought."

We believe that the sender of a communication is motivated, but we also believe that he thinks over the what-and-how contents of the message.

▲ Please return and try again.

2. The sender probably has a reason for his message and therefore sends it spontaneously with no extra to-do.

We agree this sometimes happens, but usually we tend to think over our messages before speaking. We are also thinking over what our reply will be when we are in the role of the listener. Spontaneity implies something is blurted out; normally this is not the case.

▲   Please return and select a better answer.

You answered 3: Chances are the sender of a message rehearses the message to himself before uttering one word.

This is the best choice of the three alternatives you were given.

Most of us *think over** the ideas we have before expressing them. More than likely, we rehearse to ourselves what we plan to say to somebody because we are taking into account our own role and the relationship of the idea to ourselves. Further we may even review how we will say it and go over in our minds the responses we expect to be returned to us from the receiver of our message. Undoubtedly this "plan in abstract" continues until the sender satisfies all his own questions. This concept can be illustrated this way:

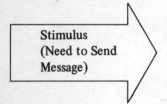

Stimulus
(Need to Send
Message)

Rehearsal *(The mind thinks about it!)*
1. To whom do we send message?
2. What exactly do we say?
3. What do we expect back as a response?

One of the few exceptions to this process is the message which is sent as a result of earlier rehearsals. By earlier rehearsals we mean a repetition of something which has been thought over for some time, evolved as an idea or conclusion, and possibly actually expressed. The listener is getting only a rerun.

---

*J. Edward Hulett, Jr., Professor of Sociology at the University of Illinois calls this process "Covert Rehearsal." (*Communication Review,* Vol. 14, Number I and Number II, Spring 1966, Summer 1967.)

Another exception is the impulsive or emotional outburst which is sent as a result of some unexpected incident which upsets the sender's normal pattern of response. We are all familiar with this type of message, and in the context of our network we could call it a short circuit.

Getting back to the mental rehearsal phenomenon, let's try to identify what in most cases is rehearsed. (During this process you can think about how *you* do it.)

1. We probably rehearse how we expect the listener to react to our message. . . . . Page 48

2. We probably do a little role-playing and mentally frame our message in terms of our understanding of our role and the listener's role. . . . . Page 49

3. Probably both (1) and (2) apply. . . . . Page 50

4. None of this goes on. We have something to say and just say it. . . . . Page 53

You answered 1: We probably rehearse how we expect the listener to react to our message.

This is partly correct.

Another ingredient was available to you in the series of questions and that was *role-playing*. We identify our listener as an enemy, a friend, interested, noninterested, a superior, etc. This means assigning him a role. After the role assignment we rehearse how we expect our message to be received.

▲   Please return and select a better answer.

2. We probably do a little role-playing and mentally frame our message in terms of our understanding of our role and the listener's role.

This is true, but you had the opportunity to include the expectations of how the listener would react to the message.

▲ Please return and choose the response which covers all the possibilities.

You chose 3: Probably both (1) and (2) apply.

You are correct.

When we understand that the sender of a message rehearses his own role and concepts, and tries to anticipate the response of the listener, we can begin to understand what communication is about.

Let us expand our illustration of the communication process this way:

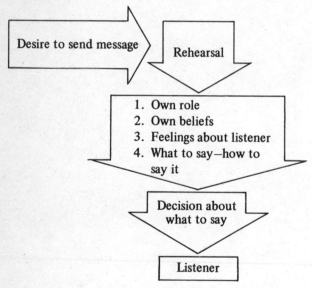

The sender tries consciously or unconsciously to identify his role. By this we mean most of us have concepts about ourselves and relate these self-concepts to our concepts of others. Our role-playing constantly changes, all in terms of

how we think we relate with the listener. For instance, a person thinks and acts differently when sending messages to a child, to a person considered as an equal, to a person with relatively less authority, to a person with relatively more authority, to a person of the opposite sex, and so forth. In other words, the tendency is to accept a role for ourselves and assign roles to others. The messages we send are often based on the role assignments we give ourselves and the listener.

When the speaker sends a message, he not only assumes a role, he reviews his concepts on the subject, and designs his approach according to his perception of the listener's role. Then he decides what's to be said and how to say it. The mind works very rapidly in these matters and can handle all these variables while the voice is saying, "Harry, do you know what . . . ?"

Once the sender makes a determination about how to send the message, he may accompany the message with certain supporting mannerisms. Thus a message may come through in a joking manner or a serious one, or perhaps it may be delivered with a scowl. These supporting mannerisms give clues to the intent behind the message.

We noted that the sender of a message makes certain assumptions about the listener. Which do you consider the more important assumption?

1. The sender of a message should understand what role he has assigned the listener.   . . . . Page 54
2. The message is going to be heard only if the listener is receptive to the message.   . . . . Page 56

You chose 4: None of this goes on. We have something to say and just say it.

If you really believe this, it is time for you to reexamine your beliefs. Just sit back and review to yourself how you go about explaining to a superior why you were late to a very important meeting. You will find yourself mentally living the situation. (You give your explanation, hear the response, make your reply.) You may try several approaches in your mind.

What we are trying to identify is the mental process which sometimes takes place before we just come out with some remark.

▲ Please return to page 47 and select another answer.

Your answer was 1: The sender of a message should understand what role he has assigned to the listener.

This is the best answer.

It is only after the sender of a message has decided on the
role of the listener that the "what to" elements of the message are addressed. Particularly when the sender of the message is concerned about the reception of the message, he casts
the listener in some kind of a role. He is quickly deciding
whether the listener is going to take an "acceptance" attitude
or perhaps a "defiant" attitude.

The listener's part, too, has been learned from childhood.
Most of us as children *learned* to respond to the desires communicated by our elders. We rehearsed to ourselves how we
would respond to a teacher, for instance, even though we
were not conscious of the process. By the time someone has
reached the point of having a job responsibility, as an average
listener, he has probably reacted to a message in a manner
similar to that illustrated on the next page.

The listener's function in the communication loop has one
basic difference beyond that of the speaker. The listener,
having received the message, usually constructs a response. In
so doing, the listener, just as the speaker, goes through a
mental rehearsal, compares roles, and so forth. But the
listener is almost always compelled to interpret the sender's
message and come to some sort of judgment or evaluation.

Now, knowing what you have learned about the speaker's
part in the communications network, select from the follow-

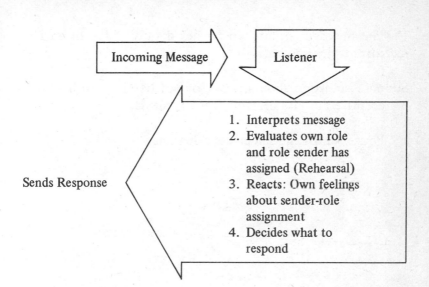

ing the best answer or answers regarding the listener's reactions when interpreting the speaker's message.

a) The listener is guided by clues such as scowls, smiles, formality of address, severity of tone, and so forth.
b) The listener responds after thinking out an answer, without considering why or how a message is spoken.
c) The listener interprets the message later when someone else's opinion can be obtained.
d) The speaker probably isn't saying *everything* he has in mind.

What would you reply?

1. The best answers are (a) and (d). . . . . . . Page 57
2. Three statements, (a), (c), and (d), apply to the question.
. . . . Page 58

2. The message is going to be heard only if the listener is receptive to the message.

Suppose someone shouts, "Get out of here!" You may not be receptive but you certainly get the message.

▲ Please return and select the other answer.

You thought 1, that statements (a) and (d) formed the best answer.

You are correct.

The listener is influenced by the clues to the message sent by the speaker. Further, most people intuitively know messages have more content than that which is sent. The speaker usually holds back something, for one reason or another. Even if this is unintentional, the speaker's mental process of figuring out what-to-send—how-to-send it implies something will be held back.

▲   Turn now to page 59.

You thought that all three statements, (a), (c), and (d), apply to this question.

Perhaps you didn't read the alternatives carefully. We are sure you will agree that it is only in special cases that we defer replying to someone's statement until we obtain someone else's opinion.

▲   Please return and consider the other answer.

We have mentioned the rapidity with which a person can rehearse the "what is to be said." The listener has the same faculty. He can rehearse a response long before the speaker has completed his message, and often does. Many conversations consist of half-spoken sentences stopped by interruptions of the listener who, anticipating the message, verbalizes a response.

Which of the following ways to receive a message describes these thoughts?

1. It probably is best to try to listen and sense what's *behind* the message, and to try to determine why the message is being sent. . . . . Page 61

2. It's wiser to try to engage your mind on the total output of the sender before rehearsing, interrupting him only if you feel you are not getting the message. . . Page 62

3. Both of these. . . . . Page 63

You answered 1. It probably is best to try to listen and sense what's behind the message, and to try to determine why the message is being sent.

This is true, but you should also feel that it is worth while to get the whole message while you are considering the possibilities of what's behind the message and the reasons it is being sent. Getting the whole message helps prevent jumping to inaccurate conclusions.

▲   Please return and try to select a better answer.

2. It's wiser to try to engage your mind with the total output of the sender before rehearsing, interrupting him only if you feel you are not getting the message.

We recommend this because giving complete attention is a part of good listening. However, it's practically impossible not to be thinking about roles, intentions, and reasons while you are hearing a person out.

▲   As there is a better answer, please return and try again.

3. Both of these.

We think this is the best answer.

Many times during conversations you will find yourself trying to respond to messages in terms of your own goals and beliefs. All of us tend to identify with our past experiences and evaluate what we hear in these terms. Much more meaning can be gleaned from a message if we just let it "come through" before allowing our pre-thought response to drown the speaker's intent.

Some sociologists think the mind also rehearses the "how" content of a message. This would mean the mind reviews not only "what to say" but also "how to say it."

We feel the mind reviews the "how to say it" content of a message only when the speaker deliberately applies importance to what attitude he wants to reflect. Most of the time the "how we say things" is woven into our personality. It is a part of our being.

Please turn now to page 64.

Here are some review questions about the communication act. The "how he's going to communicate verbally" is called the

You selected 1. Meditation.

To meditate means to ponder over something or to plan. It is possible that the speaker might meditate about his response, but we have described this mental process as rehearsing.

▲   Please continue to page 69.

1. The *content* of the communication.

No, this is wrong.

The *how* a communication is sent refers to whether we'll speak, take physical action, or use symbols. The *content* of the communication comes from what we decide to communicate and is based upon learnings and outside influences.

▲ Please turn to the questions on page 67.

You answered 2. The form the communication takes.

You are correct.

How people communicate verbally implies more than simply speaking. It can involve some action such as shaking the head, striking a table, laughing with the words, and so on. Speech might also be accompanied by illustrative symbols on paper. The *content* of a communication covers the "what" and "why" things we want to convey.

The speaker thinks about what the content of his message will contain. We have called this process

You responded with 2. Pre-message thought.

This can describe what goes on in the speaker's mind, but this is not the descriptive word we have been using. We have called the content thoughts of the speaker *rehearsal*.

▲   Please continue to page 69.

3. Rehearsal.

This is correct.

The mind goes through a sort of rehearsal before the speaker sends the message. This process gives rise to the what-and-why the speaker wants to communicate. After this point, however, the speaker is apt to mentally rehearse in words the product of his thoughts.

The rehearsal might cover such thoughts as

a) To whom do I send?
b) What words do I use?
c) What do I expect back?

Notice that item (c), "What do I expect back?" indicates that the speaker has made some assumptions about the listener. Which of the following best describes this assumption-making process?

1. The speaker thinks about the content of his message in terms of the listener's possible response. . . Page 71

2. The speaker assigns some sort of role to the listener.
. . . . Page 72

1. The speaker thinks about the content of his message in terms of the listener's possible response.

No. We think the "what do I expect back" thoughts we might have about the listener have more to do with role assignments. Let's say we assume the listener will be interested in our message. This assumption means we have assigned to him the role of an interested listener.

▲   Please continue to page 72.

2. The speaker assigns some sort of role to the listener.

Surely the better answer.

The speaker usually addresses a message in terms of what role he has assigned to the listener.

An example could be an outcry, "Do you know what you're doing!" We can be sure the speaker has decided the receiver of this message is not aware of some potential mishap. He casts the receiver in the role of an uninformed entity.

We also know through our own experiences that many times the speaker holds back, in some way, parts of what he has thought about while sending the message. Using the example again, the whole message might have been, "Do you know what you're doing, you dingaling!"

Here is our last question before proceeding to Chapter 3. As a listener, which would you feel to be the most valuable advice:

1. Try to listen to what is behind the message and to what isn't being said.   .   .   .   . Page 74
2. Mentally form a response to the message while waiting for your turn to speak.   .   .   .   . Page 75

You answered 1. Try to listen to what is behind the message and to what isn't being said.

You are correct.

Strong forces seem to be at work which compel us to want to assert our ideas, goals, identity, experience, etc., during a conversational exchange. You may find it difficult, but you should learn to be aware of the exchange of roles during conversations, and you should try to gain insights about the unexpressed portions of messages. This is not cynicism, of distrusting an individual and his motives, but a form of respect for all he feels and thinks. Demonstrating such respect will be rewarded by your own increase in communications skill.

▲   Please continue now to page 76 and Chapter 3.

2. Mentally form a response to the message while waiting for your turn to speak.

We think this normally takes place as a matter of course. Probably of more value is acquiring the faculty for determining both the reasons for messages and what might have been said but wasn't.

▲   Please turn back to page 74 and study the other answer.

the nature of intentions

A person sending a message does so with some kind of *intent*. The form and content of the message is mentally rehearsed before the message is sent on its way.

We look upon intentions as communicator-centered, that is, speaker-centered. The speaker's motives are based upon some assumption he has made about the person or persons who will be receiving his message. In other words, the speaker assumes both something about you, the listener, and something about your possible reaction to the message before he sends the message. The diagram on the next page indicates some examples.

The speaker can make all kinds of assumptions about the person to whom he is or will be speaking. The point is that the speaker (1) makes assumptions about the receiver of the message *before it is given,* and (2) makes assumptions about

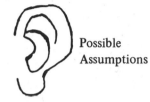

Will be interested

Will be receptive

Is going to be unreceptive

Possible
Assumptions

Will become angry

Needs to be impressed

Must take some course of action

The listener

May not take the proper course of action

what the probable reactions to the message will be *after it is given*.

This being the case, which of the following statements is correct?

a) The speaker mentally rehearses the receiver's reaction and response to his message.

b) The speaker conceives some kind of role for himself and for his receiver.

c) The speaker doesn't have time to prepare a message and also think about the possible response of the receiver.

d) The speaker thinks only of himself when preparing a message, and waits to see the receiver's reaction after the message is sent.

1. Only statements (a) and (b) are correct. . . . Page 78

2. Statements (a), (b), (c), and (d) are all correct.   Page 80

You answered 1: Only statements (a) and (b) are correct.

Excellent.

The speaker pictures himself in some sort of role. He places the receiver in a role, then mentally frames a message and anticipates a reaction to the message.

These role assignments often lead to all kinds of problems. For example, a person may feel that his position in the company entitles him to certain privileges. He assigns himself a role in keeping with this attitude and becomes very discomforted if someone else doesn't see him in the same way.

It is quite possible that some of the intentions behind a communication are influenced by the assumptions made about the receiver of the message. For instance, the speaker's intention might be to change the viewpoint of the listener. If he casts the listener in the role of a subordinate, he might take an authoritative approach to make his point. If he casts the listener in the role of a superior, he might try to persuade the listener by taking a subservient attitude. In both cases, the intent is the same but the approach taken is influenced by assumptions concerning the listener.

Unfortunately, once an individual determines on certain roles in a business situation, he tends to maintain them in his own mind. The roles weight the message content, and as a result we find faulty communication.

You may have noticed that most of what has been said here has been concerned with what the sender of a message is thinking and doing during the communication process. Suppose we reverse the situation and consider the listener or receiver of a message.

Please choose the more important of the following statements.

1. If the listener is aware of the form, content, and role assignments contained in a communication, he can make a more intelligent response.   . . . . .   Page 81
2. The listener's role is important, and the sender is aware of this when preparing his communication.   . . Page 84

1. Statements (a), (b), (c), and (d) are all correct.

This is not entirely true.

The speaker mentally rehearses the receiver's reaction and response to his message. The speaker also conceives some kind of role for himself and for his receiver.

So far, so good.

As for (c), the speaker has all kinds of time to do these things. The mind works very rapidly and can almost instantaneously consider many alternatives when forming a message. And regarding (d), the speaker's intentions force him to consider the receiver of the message.

▲   Please return and select the right answer.

1. If the listener is aware of the form, content, and role assignment contained in a communication, he can make a more intelligent response.

Certainly!

It may be that you will have to train yourself to tick these points off in your mind before responding to some communications. As you learn to do this you'll find fewer and fewer surprises, because you'll be examining what people say to you in an *analytical* manner and not in a *subjective* manner.

If you have an underlying respect for other people, you will
find it easy to learn to be analytical or objective, and your
progress with meaningful communication may be more rapid.
If you find it difficult or painful to do so, you will find it
helpful to examine your own motives.

In certain situations, an intention of a speaker can be to take
a defensive position by stretching the truth, putting on a false
front, or even lying.

Speaker's Position	Fact of the Matter
I did a great job.	The job was mediocre.
We're 80% complete.	The job is 20% complete.
I am Mr. X's assistant.	Mr. X doesn't have an assistant.

When they believe that telling the truth might place them in
an uncomfortable position, some people seem to have a
greater fear of telling the truth than do others. No one likes
to be in a position where he will be railed at, reprimanded, or
scorned. It is quite natural to want to avoid uncomfortable
situations like these. People differ as to the extent to which
they will go to avoid unpleasantness, depending on their personal standards of morality which, in turn, are based on their
total past experience.

When you discover that what someone has told you of a happening was a distortion of the truth, would you say this someone's intentions were defensive?

1. Yes.   . . . . Page 85
2. No.   . . . . Page 87

You answered 2: The listener's role is important, and the sender is aware of this when preparing his communication.

No, this is not the better of the two statements.

It does not necessarily hold that the listener's role is important to the speaker. Besides, the importance of the listener's role is only one of several items to be considered.

▲ Please return and consider the other statement.

You answered 1. Yes. You are correct.

When a person stretches the truth or exaggerates, he is taking a defensive position. His defense is against what he presumes would happen if the true facts were known.

Speaker's Position	Fact of the Matter
I did a great job.	The job was mediocre.
We're 80% complete.	The job is 20% complete.
I am Mr. X's assistant.	Mr. X doesn't have an assistant.

Let us refer again to the illustration above of the speaker's position and explain why some people take defensive positions. We all know a mediocre job brings no rewards. A great job brings recognition and perhaps other desirable outcomes.

These facts of life account for exaggerations. Work behind schedule can cost one's job. Falsifying a job completion report could buy time to bring the percentage of work completed to an acceptable level. Something might happen in another area that will make the uncompleted work less important or provide a catch-up period. Again, the listener is not aware that Mr. X doesn't have an assistant, so what's the harm? In fact, it may bring easier dealings for what the falsifier is trying to accomplish.

Another intention might be to express some expectation. Suppose after hearing the work is 80% complete, our listener now becomes a communicator. (He doesn't realize the fact is the job is only 20% complete.) Since he heard that 80% of the work is complete, he believes parts are ready for shipment to the customer and asks that a crew be available at one o'clock to start preparing these parts for shipment. However, since the bulk of the parts are not ready for shipment, the expense of a standby crew may drain away any profits that might otherwise be realized from the order.

Persons who have expectations might hope for a promise of raises, unverified acceptance and recognition, or even that falsified statements will turn out to be true. They may assign any number of outcomes to statements which are not necessarily based on fact. Which of the following do you feel is correct?

1. People with expectations probably make poor decisions.
    . . . . Page 88
2. People with expectations are like anybody else. Sometimes their decisions are right, sometimes wrong. Page 89

2. No.

This is a bad answer.

Let's look at the subject from a different angle. Let's agree some people are motivated, for example, by money or the need for security. To protect themselves, these folks avoid situations which can either embarass them or put them in jeopardy. They become defensive. The intention of a person on the defensive is to protect himself from unpleasant outcomes. Sometimes he can do this by putting the problem situation in a different light. The intention is to influence someone's point of view (behavior), and the way to do this is to paint the picture which differs somewhat from reality.

▲   Please return and select the proper answer.

1. People with expectations probably make poor decisions.

We don't really blame you for making this response. We all have expectations, and we goof once in a while. What we were trying to accomplish is to bring to you a sense of awareness about expectations which form the basis for poor decisions.

▲ Please return and select the other answer.

2. Well, I think it's probable people with expectations are like anybody else. Sometimes their decisions are right, sometimes wrong.

We think you are right on this one.

There is no reason for you to believe that a person voicing some expectation and seeking action on this expectation is making a poor decision. What is really hoped is that you will be aware that decisions based on expectations can often obscure the facts. When a person wants something to be so, he can make a decision contrary to what the facts would indicate.

Expectations are a part of everyone's life but we must be careful not to act upon expectations as if they were reality. No end of conversations will come your way which have their origin in expectations. Expectations may take the form of what someone is going to do, or what the company is going to decide, or what the customer is going to do, and so forth. While it might be possible to make some preparatory decisions based upon expectations arising from such sources, it is probably more prudent to withhold a commitment until something more substantial can support your decision.

Another intention behind a communication could be revenge. The "I'm going to get even" attitude of the child does not leave us when we become adults. It would be naive to think that people simply wouldn't do things in retaliation for a presumed or real action felt to be harmful to them. Examples of revenge might be seen in work slowdowns, deliberate sabotage of production, and negative expressions about a particular person.

Which of the following statements are examples of what might be an intent to have revenge?

a) "I don't think he deserves a raise."
b) "Why do they put up with that guy? He's always talking and never getting anything done."

Choose one of the following answers.

1. Both (a) and (b) are examples. . . . . Page 91
2. Only (a) is an example. The other sounds like gossip.
       . . . . Page 92

You answered 1: Both (a) and (b) are examples.

You are correct.

In the proper situation, either statement could be motivated by the intent to get even with somebody. We hope you observed our question said "...*what might be* an intent." It would not be proper to read into statements a revenge or retaliation intent unless you have reason to suspect a conflict between the individuals involved.

These few examples you have read expose you to the concept that it is well to listen for what might be behind a communication. The behavior of the speaker, the theme of the message, the nature of solutions to problems or the expression of problems can give clues to the speaker's intent.

We should accept the fact that most all business conversations are straightforward. Most of the time it isn't necessary to become concerned with what is behind the communication. If you feel there is more to the conversation than what is being said, you should (1) pay attention to your listening, and (2) ask questions.

Let us proceed now to some review questions.

When someone wants to communicate with you, do you believe he has made some assumptions about how you will receive his message?

1. Yes.   .   .   .   . Page 93
2. No.   .   .   .   . Page 94

You answered 2: Only (a) is an example. The other sounds like gossip.

What makes you feel gossip can't be a form of revenge? So-called "poor mouthing" a person is one of the oldest forms of revenge, and one of the hardest to compete against.

▲   Please return and consider the other answer.

You answered 1. Yes.

This is correct.

The speaker's assumption does not have to be deliberately thought out, as he might instinctively assume you will act or react in a manner he has experienced in previous conversations with you. One thing for sure, the speaker invariably has made assumptions about you and your possible reactions to the communication. Please select the correct statement from the following:

1. Role assignments depend on the content of the message.
. . . . Page 95
2. Role assignments depend on the speaker's evaluation of the listener. . . . . Page 96

You answered 2. No.

We believe a person who wants to communicate makes
certain assumptions about his audience. For example, someone might come to you for a favor. Surely, he assumes either
you will grant the favor, or will give reasons for turning down
his request. Most communications are based upon assumptions. When they aren't consciously considered, they are
taken for granted, but assumptions are made nevertheless.

▲ Review the correct answer on page 93 and continue with
the following problem.

1. Role assignments depend on the content of the message.

Just the opposite!

We feel the speaker figures out what he will say only after he has determined the role of the listener. The role he has assigned the listener influences what the contents of the message will be and how the message will be sent.

▲ Please proceed to page 96 for the next question.

2. Role assignments depend on the speaker's evaluation of the listener.

You are correct.

The content of a message gives clues as to what role the speaker has given the listener. Assigning a role is done at about the same time the speaker is rehearsing to himself the form and content of the message.

Most communications are preceded with an intention on the part of the speaker. The intention could be to air a problem, relate some facts concerning the work, or report on progress. We'll call these the plain old intentions which go along with doing a good job. There are some intentions which give clues to a speaker's desire to deliberately change our viewpoint or behavior. Some of those we discussed were based upon a person's desire for revenge, or on his expectations. Can you select from the following another intention which was discussed?

1. To lie. . . . . Page 97

2. To be defensive.   . . . . Page 98

1. To lie.

No, lying is a form of defense just as is exaggerating. To refresh your memory, we will repeat the illustration covering this subject.

Speaker's Position	Fact of the Matter
I did a great job.	The job was mediocre.
We're 80% complete.	The job is 20% complete.
I am Mr. X's assistant.	Mr. X doesn't have an assistant.

We gave examples of how the speaker in this illustration was on the defensive.

▲ Please proceed to page 99 and Chapter 4, "Opening Up Communications."

2. To be defensive.

Very good. To lie is an expression of the intent to defend oneself.

▲   Please proceed now to Chapter 4, page 99.

CHAPTER 4

opening up communications

Words by themselves have little meaning. A word's meaning comes from how what it represents has been experienced. In spoken communication, words have meaning to the message sender and to the receiver, but not necessarily the *same* meaning. Consider the statement, "The job is nearly complete." To one person this could mean half the job is finished. To another person this could mean ninety percent of the job is finished. In the latter case, just getting the job started took half the total effort required to perform the job. The other fellow was measuring from the time the job hit production, without considering planning effort, prior engineering, or setup time.

One of the roadblocks to communicating with understanding is the possibility of misinterpretation of statements. Sometimes it is necessary to find out whether a person means what you think he means. One way to do this is to restate in your own words what you think the person meant in his statement to you. When a person says, "The job is nearly finished," you might answer, "Do you mean the *whole* job or is production nearly finished?" The answer could be, "I mean the whole job—we're halfway through production already!"

What if you said, "I'm tired of answers like that. You know production started only two weeks ago—and we can't be more than half finished." Now you've turned somebody off because what he meant didn't have the same meaning for you. He was thinking of the job from beginning to end while your thoughts were on the production schedule.

Please consider the following statement and indicate your agreement or disagreement. "Because statements have a range of meanings, we must be certain at least one of the parties is in an area of understanding with the other."

1. Yes.   . . . . Page 101
2. No.   . . . . Page 102

You answered 1. Yes.

Perhaps you didn't read the statement carefully.

Because statements have a range of meanings, we must be certain *both* parties understand each other. If the statement means one thing to one of the parties and something else to the other, the conversation may not develop as it should.

▲   Please return and select the right answer.

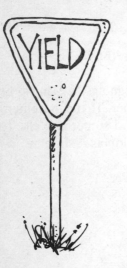

You answered 2. No.

You are correct.

You recognized that an *area of understanding* must be shared by *both* parties of a conversation. Without this shared area of understanding, misconceptions can arise and lead to bad decisions.

One way to open up conversations is to have an open mind—to realize that others do not necessarily understand exactly what you mean by what you say; nor does what they say have the same meaning for them that it has for you. This is why usually you should not take an unalterable position at the beginning of a conversation.

We're a great believer in asking questions. If a meaning isn't clear, ask questions, and let the other fellow talk back. Be sure to listen carefully to the answer.

Suppose one day Ed came into your office and blurted out, "I'm tremendously concerned about something. I've been thinking about it all week. I'm just not suited to the job you've assigned me. I've proven I'm very capable, but not on something which requires originality. I'm so serious, if I thought I could afford it, I'd quit."

Which of the following observations do you feel best describes the problem?

1. Ed is incapable.

This is not the best answer simply because you do not have
enough evidence to judge his capability. All we know is that
Ed is unhappy with his assignment. He sounds like an
achiever, and doesn't appear to be comfortable with an
assignment he cannot cope with.

▲   Please return and try again.

2. Ed has a need which is unsatisfied.

Yes indeed!

This was a fine answer. Most people want to do good work and to feel they are achieving their goals. The work assignment can become frustrating, particularly when a person knows he isn't meeting job standards or feels he isn't making progress towards a particular personal goal.

This conversation could continue or end in many ways. You could say, "I don't have time for complaints. You just keep trying. I'm sure you can do the job." Or you could say, "Look, I don't have any more assignments which haven't been filled. Do the best you can." These responses neither solve the problem nor leave the way open for further communication. It could well be that these responses were exactly what first flashed through your mind. However, in order to deal with the problem you might do better to turn the conversation *on* instead of off.

Let's examine your reactions to these thoughts. Which do you feel is correct?

1. In cases like this, it is better to go by your first reaction. . . . . Page 107
2. In cases like this, it is better to reconsider your first reaction. . . . . Page 108

Your response was to select 3. Ed is looking for an excuse to get another assignment.

Perhaps so, but from the few facts we have this doesn't appear to be so. Ed sounds like an achiever and appears to be uncomfortable with an assignment he cannot cope with.

▲   Please return and try again.

You answered 1: In cases like this, it is better to go by your first reaction.

We feel the impulse to speak out with the first thoughts which cross your mind often leads to creating problems instead of solving them. Your first reaction could be perfectly acceptable, but in most situations you will probably obtain more facts by letting the conversation develop. Encourage the man to get the problem out in the open. Listen to everything he says. Then come to a decision on how to deal with the matter.

▲   Please return and select the better answer.

You answered 2: In cases like this, it is better to reconsider your first reaction.

You are correct.

Ed was certainly upset and very serious about his viewpoint of what *to him* constituted a problem. It took a certain amount of courage for Ed to face up to the situation. If you had obeyed your first impulse, you would have turned Ed off. Your objective in situations like this should be to find out what's behind Ed's statements. There are several ways to do this. You can review Ed's assignment with him and determine where he feels incapable. You can try to find out what Ed feels he is most capable of achieving. If Ed's assignment is necessary to meeting company goals, you can point this out and try to encourage him to keep trying, and either help him yourself or help him through others.

Above all, let Ed talk! Perhaps you will learn a great deal about Ed which will guide you in helping to solve his problem or in giving him future assignments.

Another aspect of communicating deals with taking a stand about something. Let's see what happens if you take a position and make a decision that offers no alternatives.

We'll assume you have been one of three supervisors in final assembly. Your manager is transferred, and one of the other supervisors is appointed temporary manager. You don't like this, but tolerate the situation until you learn the temporary manager knows little or nothing about your operation. Furthermore, in other divisions of the firm, your operation is a separate function headed by a manager.

Suppose you decide to talk it over with the General Manager. You make an appointment, review your problem, and end up by saying, "I feel my group deserves to be made a separate department answering directly to you. If this can't be done, I'll have to quit or request a transfer to some other area."

Which of the following best describes the situation at this point?

1. The General Manager has to make a decision—whether to give your group the recognition you feel you deserve, or to try to persuade you to carry on in your present position. . . . . Page 110

2. You've given an ultimatum—the General Manager has no choice but to deny your request. . . . . . Page 111

You responded 1. The General Manager has to make a decision—whether to give your group the recognition you desire or to try to persuade you to carry on in your present position.

We are sure our astute manager will consider another alternative, and that is to deny both aspects of your request. The danger he runs by making any other decision is that of opening the doors for an endless procession of complaints and demands from others.

There is also the possibility that once he has either granted your request or persuaded you to live with the situation, he will have you again as a problem later on.

▲   Please return and choose the better answer.

2. You've given an ultimatum—the General Manager has no choice but to deny your request.

This is the better answer.

You've given the General Manager an either/or choice which is, in effect, an ultimatum, "Do as I ask or I quit." You have taken an *unalterable* position, and in most cases your request will be denied. In situations like this, it is better to bring some alternatives into the discussion. So much for that example.

It is likely that you in your own position will be confronted with ultimatums. Unpleasant as it may be, your best decision will be to point out you have been given no practicable alternatives. You must either do this or be forced to make a hard decision. If you accept the ultimatum you may be inviting further trouble by encouraging a flood of ultimatums from others.

Another way to *turn off* communications is to respond emotionally to what has been said. An excited response often kills the chance for any enlightened give-and-take. An angry response almost always does. Sometimes you cannot help making an emotional response. A series of disagreeable situations can bring us to the point where a relatively little statement sets us off into a tantrum. When this happens, it is impossible to deal rationally with the problem for several reasons.

One reason is that our normal communication link is severed. What we hear after our blowup may take the form of any number of responses, depending on the reactions of the other person. He may react in such a way that he feeds our fire of anger or he may overreact trying to soothe us. What actually happens will probably lie between these two extremes.

Another reason is that our tendency to make snap judgments seems to increase when emotions are involved. Furthermore, we are apt to say things we don't really mean.

To carry on, we'd like to ask you which of the alternatives on page 113 is more likely to open up communications.

You answered 1. Letting people disagree with me.

You are correct.

There would be little need to communicate if people all had the same viewpoint. What would there be worth talking about? We cannot assume others have our own reservoir of experience, knowledge, or values. Communication is really helped along where there is a willingness to exchange differences of opinion.

This isn't to say you should be persuaded to take some *action* you know or think is probably wrong. What it does say is that we must be receptive (not mentally belligerent) when a subordinate disagrees with our ideas, plans, or even orders.

A passing comment on this subject: When you direct a person to do something over his objections, you expect your order to be carried out. On occasion you may differ with your superior, and he may direct you to perform some action *his* way. In such a case, we hope you have made your position clear. Then you must try to do as you have been directed to, using your very best abilities.

Among our notes, there is a much underlined word, *feedback*. Feedback is probably the principal ingredient in opening up communications.

Let's take a simple example. Consider this statement, "Something's wrong with the machine." Now choose the response which will open up communication through feedback.

You answered 2. Getting people to see it my way.

There are times when it is vital to the success of a job, or even an enterprise, to insist upon doing things your own way. Our hope was that you would see through this question—because you always have the option of insisting on your way. But you cannot afford to insist constantly that work be done your way. By brushing off suggestions, objections, or even complaints, you run the risk of turning off great ideas. After a few brush-off's, your subordinates will tend to dry up. Everybody wants to be recognized, and the best recognition they can get is to be allowed to say what they think.

This is one of the key problems in communicating. It is involved with the technique of listening to others and making judgments based upon the merit of the ideas set forth. The bias of our own opinion can make us hard of hearing. Perhaps another way of saying this is that by hearing out others, we stand a better chance of getting facts or discovering usable alternatives.

▲   Please return and try the other answer.

1. Well, fix it.

Our question was, "Choose the response which will open up communications through feedback." About the only feedback you could expect from the above response is "O.K." or a blank look.

You need to know what's wrong with the equipment and how seriously the breakdown might affect your overall performance. So, "Fix it" might be the worst thing you could say.

▲   Please return and select the correct answer.

2. What do you mean, "Something's wrong with the machine"? Of course.

The basis of feedback is the giving and getting of *facts*. Did the operator damage the machine? Is only a minor adjustment required? Did a part in the machine fail? How important is the operation of the machine to the production schedule?

Getting feedback can help to bring out more than was originally intended to be said. Sometimes the whole truth is masked (not necessarily intentionally), and feedback helps remove the mask. An example is shown by this conversation. John approaches his supervisor and says, "I'm going to the technical library to see if they have anything on worm gears."

"Will you be stopping off anyplace else?" responds the supervisor.

"Well," John replies, "I thought I'd wander over to Building 81 and visit Bill. It's not really out of the way. I should be back in half an hour."

From John's first statement, do you think he intended to tell his supervisor about visiting Bill?

1. I doubt it.   .   .   .   .   Page 120

2. Sure he did. .   .   .   .   Page 122

You answered 1. I doubt it.

Perhaps you are right.

The only way we would really know this to be so is if the supervisor hadn't asked John whether he was intending to visit other places. Then if John had proceeded on his way without saying he was also going to see Bill, you'd be absolutely correct. In this example, the supervisor got additional information regardless of John's intentions.

▲   Please proceed to page 121.

We said the purpose of feedback was the giving and getting of *facts* or *information*. For feedback to have value, we must be sure we haven't assigned roles which aren't valid. It is best to "give and take" with an open mind. You could assign the role of a liar to a person and try to get feedback which brings out the truth. What if the person isn't lying? A common example is expressing an intention of doing one thing when something else (or a combination of actions) is really intended. (For example, John was going to the library, but really intended to visit with Bill.)

It is not uncommon for a person to make a statement without realizing that he isn't saying what he means. This happens particularly when a person is preoccupied. In this case, a form of feedback can be obtained by getting a person's attention when he says something which leads you to believe he isn't being too attentive to the conversation.

Now for some review questions on opening up communication, let's consider these possibilities.

Which of the following is preferred?

1. Expecting people to see things your way.   . . Page 123
2. Realizing that people don't always see things in the same way, and that it's best to seek a common ground of understanding.   .   .   .   . Page 125

You answered 2. Sure he did.

Perhaps you are right.

The only way we'd really know this to be so is if the super-visor hadn't asked John whether he was going other places, and John had continued to say that as long as he was going to the library he intended to visit Bill. In this example, the supervisor got some information regardless of John's inten-tions.

▲   Please go back to page 121.

You answered 1. Expecting people to see things your way.

You should not prefer that people see things your way until after you have given them an opportunity to differ with you, or to express viewpoints which could lead to workable alternatives. We prefer the other response which implies that you can often find a common ground of understanding, and that you might even go along with the exact opposite of your way if it proves most expedient.

▲   Please continue to page 125 for the next question.

1. It is always better to be guided by one's first reaction.

The word *always* should have tipped you off that this wasn't the right answer. You might be superstitious because you have found that your first reaction has been right more often than wrong. Consider the penalty you might incur, however, if your first reaction is wrong. From our viewpoint, it's better to repress your first reaction until you've had time to hear out the speaker.

▲   Please proceed to page 126, review the correct answer and go on with the next problem.

You answered 2. Realizing that people don't always see things in the same way, and that it's best to seek a common ground of understanding.

You are correct.

The temptation is strong to defend one's beliefs. If we can converse with an open mind, we can keep a conversation going. We should take positive attitudes when the situation warrants doing so. Many times, listening to the other fellow's viewpoints can modify our thinking and, often, another position can be better than our own. Why not admit it?

Which of the following statements is true?

1. It is always better to be guided by one's first reaction.
   . . . . Page 124
2. In some instances, it's better not to obey one's first reaction. . . . . Page 126

You selected 2. In some instances, it's better not to obey one's first reaction.

Certainly the better answer.

A great deal of misunderstanding comes about because reactions to statements are voiced before being tempered by second thoughts. Making snap decisions frequently means ignoring a choice of one of several alternatives which might be better.

We have said that taking an unalterable position on a matter does not make for good communication. Do you suppose the reason is that there is no place for the conversation to go? Or does communication come to a standstill because the other person does not have sufficiently good reasons to challenge your position?

1. The other person does not have sufficiently good reasons to challenge my position. . . . . Page 128

2. There is no place for the conversation to go.   . Page 129

You chose 1. Maintaining self-control, regardless of what
somebody else says.

This is debatable!

It isn't always easy, but it usually allows communication to
continue on a more rational level. Emotional conversations
often color the facts or simply bring further communication
to a halt.

Are conversations opened up by an exchange of viewpoints,
even when one's view disagrees with the other person's?

1. When people disagree, arguments develop. It's better to
   state and demand adherence to one's own viewpoints.
   . . . . Page 131
2. Letting people disagree lets some air into the conversational room. Demanding agreement slams the door.
   . . . . Page 132

You responded 1. The other person does not have sufficiently good reasons to challenge my position.

How can you be sure?

It is sad but true that once you take an unalterable position, the other person may as well pick up his marbles and leave. The conversation will either end or shift to another subject. If you want some give-and-take, then postpone stating your position until the time when a decision is necessary. Then make the decision. Communication is not possible when one person's mind is closed. If there is any dialogue, it will be argumentative, not exploratory.

▲   Please go back and select the other answer.

1. There is no place for the conversation to go.

You are correct.

When you take an unalterable position on a matter, the conversation might as well switch to something else. There's nothing wrong with being adamant and taking a firm stand if the situation so deserves, but you should be aware of the possible consequences.

Which of the following do you feel best keeps communication channels open?

1. Maintaining self-control, regardless of what somebody else says. . . . . Page 127
2. Being oneself—if something triggers an emotion, so be it! . . . . Page 130

You answered 2. Being oneself—if something triggers an emotion, so be it!

O.K.

We don't decry letting off steam. You should be aware that giving in to an emotional crisis can alter the way in which you would normally receive information, and it will undoubtedly curtail the amount. This is a risk you take and, if you've taken it, please learn to examine carefully the information you receive as a consequence.

▲ For the answer to the alternative approach, please turn to page 127.

1. When people disagree, arguments develop. It's better to state and demand adherence to one's own viewpoints.

This is a weak response. Getting problems out on the table where folks can discuss them and exchange viewpoints is a much more favored procedure. Having people do things your way at all times turns off any possible opportunity to tap their reservoirs of intelligence and experience.

Arguments should be controlled, but controversy should be permitted. With this policy you'll often get useful feedback. People tend to voice more when they are confident that their superior will listen with an open mind.

▲ Please proceed to page 132.

2. Letting people disagree lets some air into the conversational room. Demanding agreement slams the door.

Sure!

When you take a stand which does not allow an exchange of viewpoints, the conversation is closed. While there are occasions when an exchange of viewpoints serves no purpose, you should be aware that a closed position allows for no expansion of views or ideas. Even apparently unlikely ideas turned up in brainstorming sessions often yield new points of view.

Incidentally, which of the following did we say was the purpose of feedback?

1. Letting people *disagree* with me.   .   .   . Page 133
2. Giving and getting *facts*.   .   .   .   .   .   . Page 134

1. Letting people *disagree* with me.

No, we think you are confusing this question with some of the other ways of opening up communications. Feedback is a way of getting facts. When someone makes a statement you don't quite follow, you can ask questions aimed at getting clarification—this provides one kind of feedback.

Or you may give some instructions and then ask for your instructions to be repeated to you to make sure you were understood. During the playback you may find that the other person doesn't grasp exactly what you have said. This kind of *feedback* helps you to know where to elaborate on your instructions so that you can eliminate possible errors.

▲ Please go to page 134.

2. Giving and getting *facts*.

Very good.

The purpose of feedback is the giving and getting of facts. This is the underlying purpose of the communication exchange. Feedback among other things, uncovers masked intents, gets attention, and tends to clarify differences of opinions or misunderstandings about what is being related.

Now please proceed to page 135 and Chapter 5, "Gateways."

•

CHAPTER 5

gateways

All through recorded history, we find examples of people who, by either their appearance or their deeds, set themselves off from others. Nero, we are told, played the lyre while Rome burned. George Sand, a brilliant woman, sometimes dressed in a man's garb and smoked big, black cigars—in an age when such behavior shocked society. Based upon historical impressions, we might be tempted to say one was an egomaniac and the other a sensation seeker. If we knew nothing about what history records about them and could meet with them face to face, however, we might be utterly *charmed.*

In a sense, we are conditioned by what we believe or know about a person, and we tend to pre-judge in adopting our attitude toward any given individual. When someone comes to us for a decision, our response to his petition may be influenced (unbeknownst to him) by what we think about his

role. We can consider this person either a "nothing," a "somebody," a "lazy one," a "promoter," a "driver," and so forth.

Which statement is more important?

1. We have to be careful in our pre-judging if we are to make good decisions.   .   .   .   . Page 138

2. We have to defer judgment when a person is com-municating with us.   .   .   .   . Page 139

You responded 1. No.

You are correct.

We have a natural tendency to evaluate statements for ourselves. We are going to agree with some statements, and we are going to disagree with or disapprove of other statements.

Now let's carry this thought a step further.

Which of the following *extends* what we have been discussing?

1. In some cases, conversations become more meaningful when the evaluation tendency is delayed.   . . Page 141

2. It really doesn't matter whether conversations are allowed to continue, so long as we keep sight of and act upon our initial judgments. . . . . Page 143

3. One's experience should dictate what's right or wrong in most situations.   . . . . Page 144

You chose 1. We have to be careful in our pre-judging if we are to make good decisions.

We rather hoped our example made it clear this was precisely what you should *not* want to do. Pre-judgments have a tendency to turn away the truth. There is probably something akin between pre-judgments and first reactions, perhaps because neither allows an opportunity to determine whether our reactions represent the best solution.

▲ Please return and try the other answer.

You answered 2. We have to defer judgment when a person is communicating with us.

Exactly!

We have a natural tendency to cast people in roles, and to judge or evaluate immediately the communications brought to us. It is not easy to defer judgment. Our tendency to judge is from a personal point of reference, one based on our own observations and conclusions, or one influenced by someone with whom we have associated, such as a parent, teacher, associate, or other figure important in shaping our attitudes.

Too hasty decisions, if they are not based on careful consideration, turn off people's creativity. It is usually the case that judgments effectively create a communication barrier. Another interesting observation is that hasty personal judgments seem to increase to a greater degree than normal when our emotions are involved.

Supposing we said, "People believe and accept the statements of others." Would you agree with this statement?

1. No.   . . . . Page 137
2. Yes.   . . . . Page 140

You answered 2. Yes.

This question is a very positive one: "People *believe* and *accept* the statements of others." In Chapter 1 we said that people *tend* to believe what they hear. By now you should realize that we accept a role for ourselves and for the other person. Perhaps when roles are not clearly identified or are not accepted—if identified—is when we challenge what we hear.

Think back on some of your most recent conversations—surely you didn't believe everything said to you. The conversational give-and-take between people allows for a great deal of debate and differences of opinion. We feel you will agree that people tend to accept some statements made by others; they don't believe and accept all the statements.

▲   Please return and try the other response.

1. In some cases, conversations become more meaningful when the evaluation tendency is delayed.

You are correct. This is certainly the best answer.

One way we can take a "delayed judgment" posture is by putting ourselves in the other person's shoes! Trying to use the other person's frame of reference can be rewarding.

Business communications follow many channels. We become very frustrated when we order a thing and receive something entirely different because of faulty communication. When we are giving orders or instructions, many courses of feedback are available and should be used. When someone brings us a communication, chances are the deferred judgment theory also applies. Furthermore, sometimes when a person relates something disturbing to us, we find on further examination that the apparent threat is really quite harmless.

Exercising deferred judgment requires that we make a real effort to *listen* to a communication without (1) jumping to a conclusion, (2) pre-judging from our own frame of reference, or (3) evaluating the message on an emotional basis. We must develop patience, even though it may mean unlearning what we may have become accustomed to do in response to a communication.

Please try to remember this: *Most people with expertise about person-to-person dialogue agree that an individual's personal evaluation tendency constitutes a major barrier to meaningful communication.*

This brings us to the subject of listening. You know now
that the act of communication consists of a sender and a
receiver. The receiver is, by definition, a listener—or should
be! Believe it or not, there are two ways of going about
listening. We call these simply listening and nonlistening.

Which of the following applies to you?

1. My listening is personal—I either identify with the
   speaker or turn myself off.   .   .   .   .   .   Page 145
2. I listen, man!   .   .   .   .   Page 146

2. It really doesn't matter whether conversations are allowed to continue, so long as we keep sight of and act upon our initial judgments.

This is not right. Were you just guessing?

The point of letting conversations continue is to bring out facts which might lead us to modify or change our initial judgments.

▲   Please return and try again.

3. One's experience should dictate what's right or wrong in most situations.

Perhaps this is true, but it infers that you prefer to let your experience dictate a decision rather than deferring judgment until you've listened to whatever ideas may be offered by others. Your position is not in line with the best practice.

▲   Please return and try again.

You answered 1. My listening is personal—I either identify with the speaker or turn myself off.

This is a good and honest answer.

A person listens when he's interested in what the speaker is saying. He can turn himself off. Turning off often happens when we decide we know more than the speaker does about the subject, or when we get bored because we don't really care about what he is saying, or for many other reasons. We may have something more urgent or interesting to do or we may find ourselves getting angry because the speaker is taking a position on a subject which outrages our personal views.

In any case, we hope you agree one can listen or nonlisten, depending upon an internal evaluation of the speaker and/or the message.

▲ Please proceed to page 147.

You answered 2. I listen, man!

Fine enough!

A person can listen when he's interested in what the speaker has to say. It takes a great deal of discipline to listen when the speaker's viewpoint tends to "turn us off."

It is commendable when, in spite of differing viewpoints, a person learns to really listen to another. If this is why you chose this response, you are doubly commended.

▲   Please proceed to page 147.

You probably have agreed by now that the component—listening—is relevant to effective communication. Some folks have learned to exclude their personal views when they listen. They do not pre-judge; they listen in the hope of gaining new insights, information which will either reenforce what they already believe, or enable them to modify their own beliefs toward what may possibly be a wiser posture.

Others, of course, take the position that they alone have all the relevant facts about the situation and the capacity to make no mistakes in their decisions. With these people, the speaker either reenforces their beliefs, or he finds that the listener has ceased to listen. There are other reasons for non-listening. The listener may be just plain weary, distracted, or emotionally upset, or he may be under a nearly intolerable

amount of pressure. These conditions are, of course, sometimes unavoidable, but a wise manager will recognize the source of and the tendency to nonlistening both in himself and in others. He will take such factors into consideration if decision-making is necessary.

Please select the statement you feel is more nearly accurate.

1. Listening can become a problem when the speaker talks too much. . . . . Page 149

2. Listening can become a problem when we have made accurate role assignments. . . . . . . Page 151

1. Listening can become a problem when the speaker talks too much.

This is a good response.

Some people just have to talk, and in some cases seem to be compulsive about talking. They have what we might call a push of speech. So, being a good listener is commendable. However, we must learn to sense when our listening encourages someone to speak on and on . . . and on. When this appears to be happening, it is better to bring the subject into focus, even if abrupt treatment is required.

There are other times when we are faced with listening to somebody whose role we have inaccurately assigned. We are sometimes led to believe a person is an expert on some subject only to realize that actually we know more about the subject than he does. Or perhaps someone's conduct or his abuse of language destroys our previous concepts about him. In these cases, the tendency is for us to turn off our listening. We may become defensive or want to retaliate in some way. We should temper our judgment and pay attention to what the person is saying. We make this recommendation because, more than likely, there was some basis for our original casting of roles. If there was, we stand to learn something by being patient.

Suppose you accept the fact that the mind operates at a very high speed when compared to the speed with which someone's words arrive through the listening senses. Then which of the following statements is true?

You answered 2. Listening can become a problem when we
have made accurate role assignments.

If our assessment of a speaker is accurate, we usually do not
have a listening problem because we know what to expect. If
we figure someone is a bore and he proceeds to be boring, we
could, of course, have a listening problem, that is, unless we
have made an accurate role assignment and done something
about it.

▲   Please return and try the other answer.

1. I have no spare time to think when someone is speaking to me.

If you give your attention to the conversation, you will have loads of spare time to think. This excess of time to think is one of the problems in maintaining meaningful communication. If the speaker doesn't hold your attention, your mind wanders. Or you may grasp the meaning of the communication long before the speaker has finished, and you may be thinking of your response. Either situation indicates that you do have the spare time after all.

▲ Please return and try the other answer.

You answered 2: I can think ahead of the speaker and try to determine where all this talking is leading me.

Yes, this is the correct response.

All of us have experienced times when inwardly we feel the other fellow will never get to his point, one which we arrived at eons ago during his monologue. It is well to remember that you can learn to use spare thinking time profitably during conversations. You can weigh the evidence, you can listen in a sense to what's not being said, and you can search out in your mind evidence which supports ideas—yours or his.

It is obvious that *good listening* is a skill which requires one's intelligent efforts. To listen with willingness is of great importance to personal communication. This is a faculty which when developed will open many doors leading to the acceptance and understanding of others.

Finally, if you can establish an exchange of acceptances, you will have developed a freedom of outlook which cannot exist in a "closed mind" environment. A decision for action is bound to be better when all avenues of approach have been explored. If only *your* personal knowledge and *your* personal ideas are the basis for action-type decisions, you may some day make a grievous decision directly attributed to a lack of communication exchange.

We are not going to quiz you upon this chapter, but ask that you read the Summary which starts on the following page.

CHAPTER 6

summary

After all this work, it is time to sum up what we have learned. The primary premise is that most decisions are expressed verbally. Because most day-to-day decisions are communicated this way, the verbal decision-making process has a large, but unmeasurable, impact upon the entire conduct of the business. Therefore, each of us all should make a real effort to understand the various elements of "verbal communication" and how these elements affect the decision-making process.

We have addressed ourselves to the business aspects of communicating, not the social kind of give-and-take. One of our first observations was that behind practically all communications was some kind of intention. When a person singles you out as the one to whom he will deliver a message, you should make the natural assumption that he has a reason (or intent)

behind his message. Here are some examples of what we describe as intentions:

To find the "truth"
To change the other person's behavior
To obtain feedback
To persuade (his way!—some way!).

The communication between two persons has a *sender-receiver* relationship. An awareness of what is really transpiring during the dialogue between one person and another is the essential basis for understanding the communication process. When someone decides to communicate, a series of events takes place. You must realize that the probability is strong that those communication sequences are happening. Such a realization will reenforce your ability to comprehend the message. It is equally important to understand what is *not* being communicated.

These communication sequences have been simplified by dividing the desire to communicate into two elements. These elements consist of the *form* and the *content* of the communication. A communication can take place in one of three forms: (1) through actions, (2) through speaking, or (3) through the use (or application) of symbols. The content of the message is based on the resources of one's experiences (belief state), usually modified by intentions and outside influences. It is obvious that much of the what is said and how it is said can be more readily understood if an insight to the appropriate contents of the individual's experience reservoir can be obtained.

An interesting phenomenon is that most communications are rehearsed. The rehearsal is a mental act: The mind goes over what is to be said, how it will be said, probable responses, the speaker's and listener's roles (as the speaker envisions them), etc. The assignment of roles has much to do with both the form and content of a message. Once this has been decided, the rest of the rehearsal is conditioned. The way the sender sees his own role and the role of the receiver influences what he says, how he says it, and consequently how the other person interprets his attitude and meaning.

The listener has time to rehearse also. While a message is being conveyed, the listener anticipates (1) the content of the message, (2) analyzes and reacts to the roles which the speaker seems to have assigned, and (3) rehearses an answer. A good listener also has time to consider possible ramifications about what was not said, for one reason or another, by the speaker.

There seems to be an interrelation between intentions, assumptions, and role assignments. For instance, the speaker's intention might be to impress you with his knowledge about a certain subject. Let's say he also *assumes* you will be receptive and need to be impressed. He may want to impress you to reenforce his own need for a feeling of superiority, or he may simply be trying to establish himself, as an expert on the subject matter. He assigns roles based upon his evaluation of you as either superior, peer, or subordinate. If he is wise and experienced, he sends the message in a manner most likely to be accepted by you in one of these roles. Role assignments which are inappropriate can make the listener feel he is being talked down to or, on the other hand, is being insincerely flattered, either of which can lead to anger or mistrust.

Intentions can arise as a result of outside pressures which place the speaker in a defensive position. Being on the defensive causes some people to stretch the truth or make a deliberate misrepresentation. Outside pressures can be created, for example, by over-running the budget, falling behind in the work schedule, or perhaps by declining sales caused by over-pricing of company products or underpricing by competitors. Such situations often arise, and it is the astute supervisor who early in the game encourages problem-solving by making an honest effort to get problems out in the open and deal with them in honest, aboveboard ways. If you detect a defensive posture by someone's "explaining the situation," by all means search for the facts—don't settle for anything less.

We all have expectations which can lead us into slumberland. We want the work to be on time, properly done, and we want just rewards for the part we play in successful production. Our associates are no different. Some need to be convinced that it is better to deal with the facts of the situation rather than to cling to unrealistic expectations. The extension of expectations built upon facts or purposeful desire can be worth while, of course, and worthy of recognition and en-couragement. It is up to the supervisor to make this some-times difficult discrimination.

Words and statements can have a range of meanings. The computer scientist, explaining to the layman the components of a problem, is often misunderstood. This same scientist, speaking to another computer scientist, can communicate his reasoning precisely. Putting the message into words under-standable by the layman may lessen the preciseness of the message. What's the best solution to these situations? Although the process is often a laborious and frustrating one to the expert, it is wise for him to work out carefully a common ground of understanding.

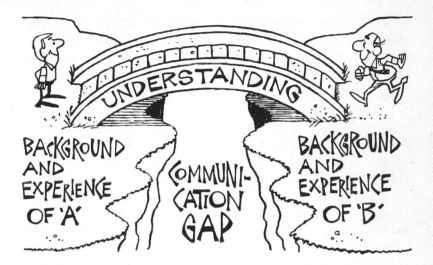

We realize, of course, that people have different ways of acting upon such things as job assignments or reporting activities. Sometimes it becomes both difficult and costly to bridge the communication gap created by our different backgrounds and experiences. It is not uncommon for people who have grown up together and been noted as close friends, to have a falling out because they misunderstood each other and suddenly couldn't communicate. Even though the area of communication is more limited in business relationships, this difficulty in understanding and communicating is magnified with the more superficial relationships we develop in our work roles.

It is wise, therefore, to listen carefully to what is being said
and above all else, to avoid taking an *unalterable position.*
Further, it is equally wise most often not to obey first impulses. You may have noticed we said, "most often." There
are no hard and fast rules in these matters. Suppose you do
act upon the initial reaction to a message? Chances are this is
a good decision. But you always have the option of making
your first reaction decision *after* you have taken the time to
mull over this and possible alternatives. Keeping control of
the situation is the better method.

Unalterable positions can prove to be very troublesome. It is
better to avoid them unless you find yourself with no other
recourse. If you give an ultimatum or take an either/or position, you will have no leeway for compromises or alternatives.

Every now and then circumstances place us in a position
which stretches our tolerance and our patience. All of us have
been there, and, to use the vernacular, lost our cool. When
your patience is being stretched beyond its normal limits
(and usually your experience will give you ample warning
when this tolerance point is reached), it is best to take com-
mand. You can always be in control if you, in fact, control
yourself. Emotional outbursts and letting off steam can be
very therapeutic under some conditions, but are seldom
appropriate in a business situation. If you are going to let
yourself go, be sure you have a very good reason for the
outburst. You may be putting yourself at a disadvantage in
terms of respect, because emotional statements usually are
unnecessary and are apt to be strongly biased your way. One
fact is certain, moreover, if you allow yourself to blow off

steam, you will have *turned off* meaningful communication, at least for the time being.

Many of us find confrontations distasteful, so our natural tendency is to avoid them, but good decisions are hard to make and cooperation is difficult to maintain if we don't understand all aspects of a problem. We should avoid situations which are fraught with misunderstandings or disagreements. In such cases, it pays to encourage our people to discuss what *they* feel should be said or done. Necessary controversy should always take place in an atmosphere in

which the participants feel comfortable and are without fear
of reprisals or retaliation. A supervisor who cannot achieve
this kind of understanding with his workers will be locked
into a "yes, sir—no, sir" environment.

We believe good decisions can be made only if we can depend
on the reliability of what has been communicated. In order
to obtain this assurance, we often seek *feedback*. Now just
what does feedback do? It gives us some assurance that what
we believe we hear from others, what we accept as facts, and
what we consequently use as a basis for our decisions are
based on a clear line of communication. It also assures us
about how clearly others understand the basic meaning of
what we are trying to get across.

It is most unusual to find two people who see things exactly
alike. In the first place, no two of us have identical learning
experiences, and our judgments are influenced by what we
have learned to believe. Some of our decisions are based upon
what we think we heard someone tell us. Such communication obviously is influenced by a person's belief state and his
ability to hear (or listen to) what is being related. In many
cases the reliability of statements upon which we may have
to make quick decisions must be checked through utilizing
feedback.

It is clear that we must develop the ability to listen—listen
with much patience. Only in this way can we detect what is
behind a message. We must develop the ability to determine
not only the value of what *is* being said, we must be sensitive
to what *is not* being said. During all the listening we will have
time to frame our response and weigh a few pros and cons.

We will have time to think of the roles involved and the reaction to the speaker's role-casting (if it applies). Careful and sensitive listening is probably the most important key to intelligent decision-making through the verbal communication process.

A thing to avoid during the listening process is the tendency to make personal evaluations, because such evaluations are largely influenced by what roles we assign the speaker. If a subordinate makes a statement we are less inclined to listen than we are if a superior does. We should try to tune in to any person who directs a communication to us. It is *always* rewarding for the person to whom you are listening when you are attentive to his message. People have a feel for, or a way of knowing, the level of attention they are getting from their communication. By not listening, you can turn someone off. If you don't get the whole message, you may be depriving yourself of facts necessary for the best possible decision.

Decision-making, based upon verbal communications, is influenced by our level of confidence in the communication. Some of us have the tendency to hear something, make a decision, and act upon it. We don't necessarily fault such actions, particularly when time is of the essence. When time permits, we advocate a policy of deferred judgment.

To recapitulate then, there are many instances when a message is delivered which seems to demand a forthright decision and immediate action. In our experience very few of these situations are critically urgent. You do have time to weigh your decision. Various alternatives may be available to you. You should back off from the apparent urgency of the situation and evaluate the facts as you understand them.

Learning to defer judgment can be very rewarding. It helps you to control impulses, to get and examine as many facts as possible, to consider various alternatives, and to make a well-balanced decision.

This concludes our remarks. We hope you have found this text useful and that some gateways for expanded communication skills have been opened for you.

ABCDE79876543210